Walt Disney Pictures Presents

Aladdin

ILLUSTRATED SONGBOOK

ISBN 0-7935-3412-7

HAL•LEONARD
CORPORATION
7777 W. BLUEMOUND RD. P.O. BOX 13819 MILWAUKEE, WI 53213

© The Walt Disney Company

Walt Disney Pictures Presents

Aladdin

ILLUSTRATED SONGBOOK

Arabian Nights

Arabian Nights

Moderately bright

Lyrics by **Howard Ashman**
Music by **Alan Menken**

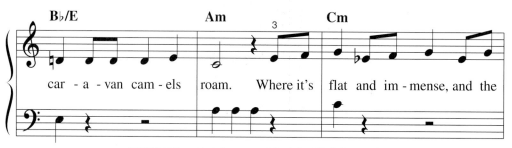

Narrator: Oh, I come from a land, from a far a - way place where the car - a - van cam - els roam. Where it's flat and im - mense, and the

please turn the page . . .

7

Arabian Nights

Lyrics by **Howard Ashman** • Music by **Alan Menken**

Narrator: Oh, I come from a land, from a far away place
Where the caravan camels roam.
Where it's flat and immense, and the heat is intense.
It's barbaric, but hey, it's home.
When the wind's from the east and the sun's from the west
And the sand in the glass is right.
Come on down, stop on by, hop a carpet and fly
To another Arabian night.
Arabian nights like Arabian days
More often than not are hotter than hot in a lotta good ways.
Arabian nights 'neath Arabian moons,
A fool off his guard could fall and fall hard
Out there on the dunes.

One Jump Ahead

One Jump Ahead

Music by **Alan Menken**
Lyrics by **Tim Rice**

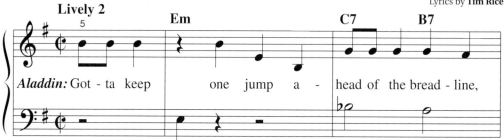

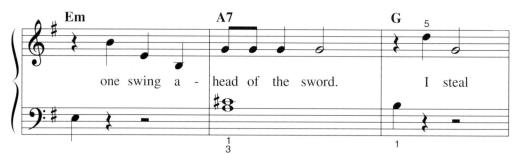

One Jump Ahead

Music by **Alan Menken** • Lyrics by **Tim Rice**

Aladdin: Gotta keep one jump ahead of the breadline,
One swing ahead of the sword.
I steal only what I can't afford.
(Spoken:) *That's everything!*
One jump ahead of the lawmen.
That's all, and that's no joke.
These guys don't appreciate I'm broke.

Crowd: Riff raff! Street rat! Scoundrel! Take that!

Aladdin: Just a little snack, guys.

Crowd: Rip him open, take it back, guys.

Aladdin: I can take a hint, gotta face the facts.
You're my only friend, Abu!

Crowd: Who?

Ladies: Oh it's sad Aladdin's hit the bottom.
He's become a one man rise in crime.
I'd blame parents except he hasn't got 'em.

Aladdin: Gotta eat to live, gotta steal to eat,
Tell you all about it when I got the time!
One jump ahead of the slowpokes,
One skip ahead of my doom.
Next time gonna use a nom-de-plume.
One jump ahead of the hitmen,

One hit ahead of the flock.
I think I'll take a stroll around the block.

Crowd: Stop thief! Vandal! Outrage! Scandal!

Aladdin: Let's not be too hasty.

Lady: Still I think he's rather tasty.

Aladdin: Gotta eat to live, gotta steal to eat,
Otherwise we'd get along.

Crowd: (Spoken:) *Wrong!*

Aladdin: One jump ahead of the hoofbeats.

Crowd: Vandal!

Aladdin: One hop ahead of the hump.

Crowd: Street rat!

Aladdin: One trick ahead of disaster.

Crowd: Scoundrel!

Aladdin: They're quick but I'm much faster.

Crowd: Take that!

Aladdin: Here goes. Better throw my hand in.
Wish me happy landin'.
All I gotta do is jump!

One Jump Ahead (Reprise)

One Jump Ahead
(Reprise)

Music by **Alan Menken**
Lyrics by **Tim Rice**

One Jump Ahead (Reprise)

Music by **Alan Menken**
Lyrics by **Tim Rice**

Aladdin: Riff raff, street rat,
I don't buy that.
If only they'd look closer,
Would they see a poor boy?
No siree.
They'd find out
There's so much more to me.

Friend Like Me

Friend Like Me

Lyrics by **Howard Ashman**
Music by **Alan Menken**

F7

pride   our - selves   on   ser - vice.   You're the

Am

boss,   the   king,   the   shah.   Say

F7

what   you   wish.   It's   yours!   True   dish how 'bout a

Dm　　　　　　　　　　　　　　　　　　　**E7**   **D.C. al Coda**

lit - tle more   bak - la - va? _____

please turn the page . . .

CODA

C/G

nev - er had a friend, nev - er had a friend, you ain't

Ab7

nev - er had a friend, nev - er had a friend. You ain't

F7b5

nev - er had a

Esus   E7   Am

friend   like   me.

24

Friend Like Me

Lyrics by **Howard Ashman** • Music by **Alan Menken**

Genie: Well, Ali Baba had them forty thieves.
Scheherazade had a thousand tales.
But, master, you in luck 'cause up your sleeves
You got a brand of magic never fails.
You got some power in your corner now,
Some heavy ammunition in your camp.
You got some punch, pizazz, yahoo and how.
See, all you gotta do is rub that lamp.
And I'll say, Mister Aladdin, sir,
What will your pleasure be?
Let me take your order, jot it down.
You ain't never had a friend like me. No no no.
Life is your restaurant and I'm your maitre d'.
C'mon whisper what it is you want.
You ain't never had a friend like me.
Yes sir, we pride ourselves on service.
You're the boss, the king, the shah.
Say what you wish. It's yours!
True dish, how 'bout a little more baklava?
Have some of column "A".
Try all of column "B".
I'm in the mood to help you, dude,
You ain't never had a friend like me.
Wa-ah-ah. Oh my.
Wa-ah-ah. No no.

Wah-ah-ah. Na na na.
Can your friends do this?
Can your friends do that?
Can your friends pull this out their little hat?
Can your friends go poof!
(Spoken:) *Well, looky here.*
Can your friends go abracadabra,
Let 'er rip and then make the sucker disappear?
So doncha sit there slack jawed, buggy eyed.
I'm here to answer all your midday prayers.
You got me bonafide certified.
You got a genie for your chargé d'affaires.
I got a powerful urge to help you out.
So whatcha wish I really want to know.
You got a list that's three miles long, no doubt.
Well, all you gotta do is rub like so. And oh.
Mister Aladdin, sir, have a wish or two or three.
I'm on the job, you big nabob.
You ain't never had a friend, never had a friend,
You ain't never had a friend, never had a friend.
You ain't never had a friend like me.
Wa-ah-ah. Wa-ah-ah.
You ain't never had a friend like me. Ha!

Prince Ali

Prince Ali

Lyrics by **Howard Ashman**
Music by **Alan Menken**

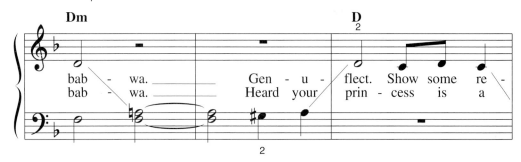

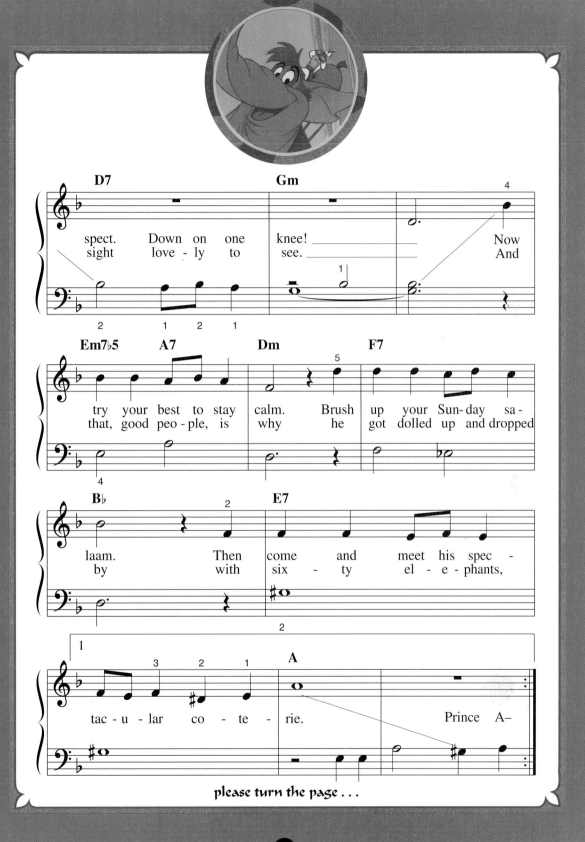

please turn the page . . .

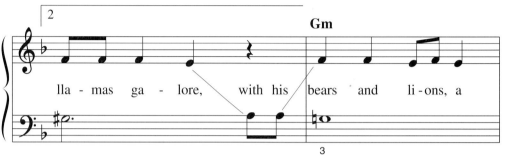

Gm

lla - mas ga - lore, with his bears and li - ons, a

Dm

brass band and more. With his for - ty fa - kirs, his

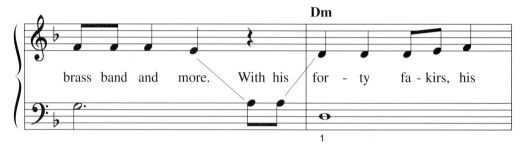

Dm/C   **Dm/B**

cooks, his bak - ers, his birds that war - ble on

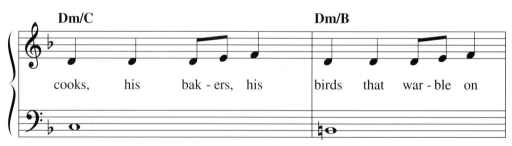

B♭7   **Dm/A**

key. Make way _____ for

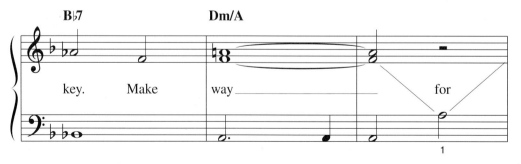

Prince A - li!

Prince Ali

Lyrics by **Howard Ashman** • Music by **Alan Menken**

Chorus: Make way for Prince Ali.
Say hey, it's Prince Ali.

Genie: Hey! Clear the way in the old Bazaar.
Hey you! Let us through!
It's a bright new star!
Oh, come be the first on your block
To meet his eye.
Make way, here he comes!
Ring bells. Bang the drums!
Are you gonna love this guy!
Prince Ali! Fabulous he! Ali Ababwa.
Genuflect. Show some respect.
Down on one knee!
Now try your best to stay calm.
Brush up your Sunday salaam.
Then come and meet his spectacular coterie.
Prince Ali! Mighty is he! Ali Ababwa.
Strong as ten regular men definitely.
He faced the galloping hordes,
A hundred bad guys with swords.
Who sent those goons to their Lords?
Why, Prince Ali.

Chorus: He's got seventy-five golden camels.

Genie: (Spoken:) *Don't they look lovely, June?*

Chorus: Purple peacocks, he's got fifty-three.

Genie: (Spoken:) *Fabulous, Harry, I love the feathers.*

Chorus: When it comes to exotic type mammals,
Has he got a zoo?
I'm telling you, it's a world class menagerie.

Genie: Prince Ali, handsome is he,

Chorus: There's no question this Ali's alluring.

Genie: Ali Ababwa.

Chorus: Never ordinary, never boring.

Genie: That physique! How can I speak?
Weak at the knee.

Chorus: Ev'rything about the man just plain impresses.

Genie: Well, get on out in that square.

Chorus: He's a winner, he's a whiz, a wonder.

Genie: Adjust your veil and prepare

Chorus: He's about to pull my heart asunder.

Genie: To gawk and grovel and stare at Prince Ali.

Chorus: And I absolutely love the way he dresses.
He's got ninety-five white Persian monkeys.
He's got the monkeys. Let's see the monkeys.
And to view them he charges no fee.
He's generous. So generous.
He's got slaves, he's got servants and flunkies.
Proud to work for him, bow to his whim,
Love serving him.
They're just lousy with loyalty to Ali!
Prince Ali!

Chorus & Genie: Prince Ali! Amorous he! Ali Ababwa.

Genie: Hear your princess was a sight lovely to see.
And that, good people, is why he got dolled up
And dropped by

Chorus: With sixty elephants, llamas galore,
With his bears and lions, a brass band and more.
With his forty fakirs, his cooks, his bakers,
His birds that warble on key.
Make way for Prince Ali!

A Whole New World

A Whole New World

Sweetly

Music by **Alan Menken**
Lyrics by **Tim Rice**

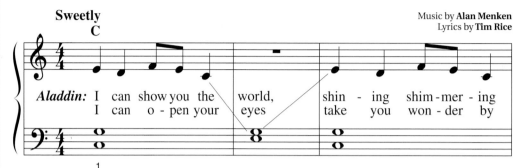

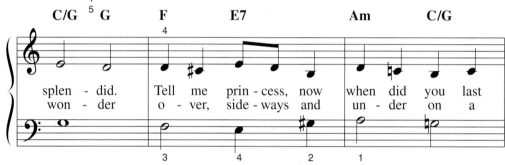

Aladdin: I can show you the world, shin - ing shim - mer - ing
I can o - pen your eyes take you won - der by

splen - did. Tell me prin - cess, now when did you last
won - der o - ver, side - ways and un - der on a

please turn the page . . .

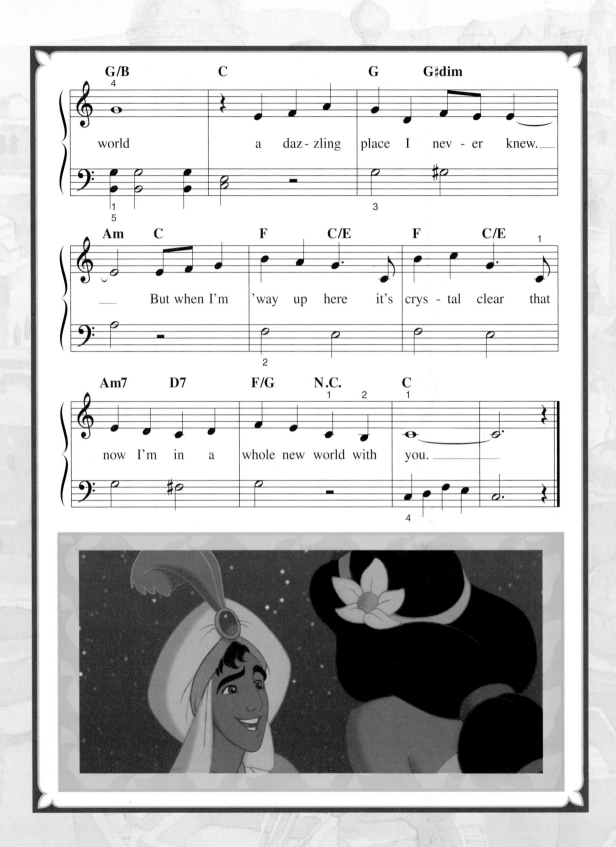

world   a daz-zling place I nev-er knew.

But when I'm 'way up here it's crys-tal clear that

now I'm in a whole new world with you.

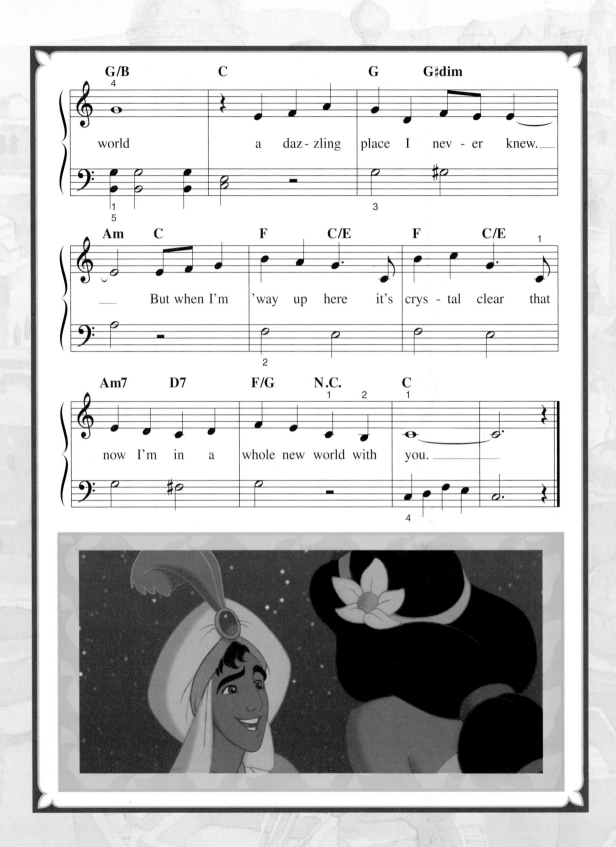

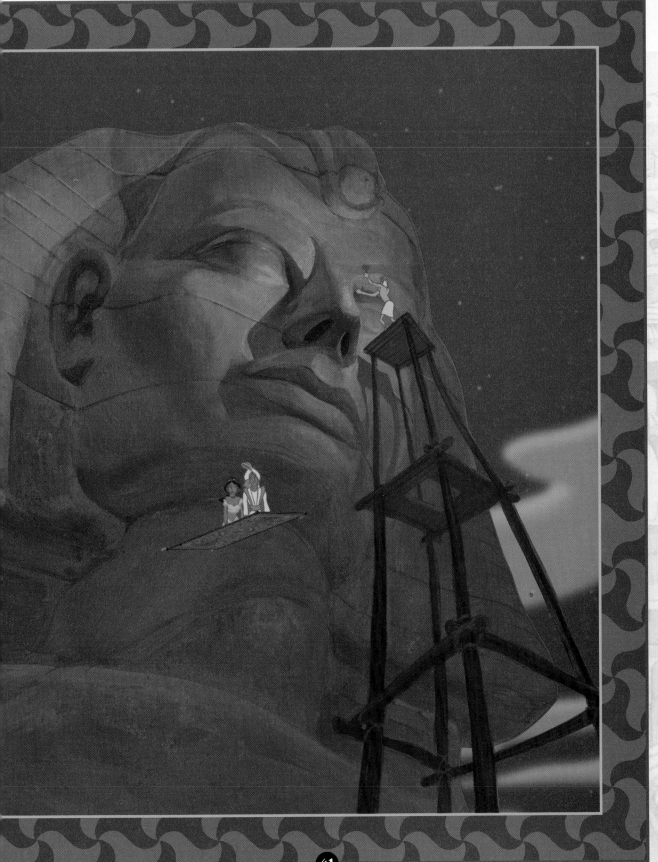

A Whole New World

Music by **Alan Menken** • Lyrics by **Tim Rice**

Aladdin: I can show you the world,
                Shining, shimmering, splendid.
                Tell me princess, now
                When did you last let your heart decide?
                I can open your eyes
                Take you wonder by wonder
                Over, sideways and under on a magic carpet
                ride.
                A whole new world,
                A new fantastic point of view.
                No one to tell us no or where to go
                Or say we're only dreaming.

Jasmine: A whole new world,
                A dazzling place I never knew.
                But when I'm way up here it's crystal clear
                That now I'm in a whole new world with you.

Aladdin: Now I'm in a whole new world with you.

Jasmine: Unbelievable sights, indescribable feeling.
                Soaring, tumbling, free-wheeling
                Through an endless diamond sky.
                A whole new world,

Aladdin: Don't you dare close your eyes.

Jasmine: A hundred thousand things to see.

Aladdin: Hold your breath, it gets better.

Jasmine: I'm like a shooting star I've come so far
                I can't go back to where I used to be.

Aladdin: A whole new world.

Jasmine: Every turn a surprise.

Aladdin: With new horizons to pursue.

Jasmine: Ev'ry moment red-letter.

Both: I'll chase them anywhere. There's time to spare.
                Let me share this whole new world with you.

Aladdin: A whole new world,

Jasmine: A whole new world,

Aladdin: That's where we'll be.

Jasmine: That's where we'll be.

Aladdin: A thrilling chase

Jasmine: A wond'rous place

Both: For you and me.

Prince Ali
(Reprise)

Prince Ali
(Reprise)

Music by **Alan Menken**
Lyrics by **Tim Rice**

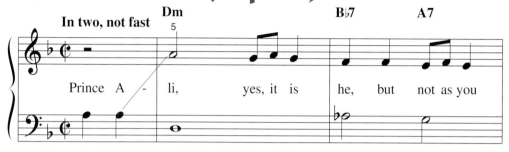

Prince A - li, yes, it is he, but not as you

know him. Read my lips and come to

Prince Ali (Reprise)

Music by **Alan Menken** • Lyrics by **Tim Rice**

Jafar: Prince Ali, yes, it is he,
But not as you know him.
Read my lips and come to grips with reality.
Yes, meet a blast from your past
Whose lies were too good to last.
Say hello to your precious Prince Ali!
So Ali turns out to be merely Aladdin.
Just a con, need I go on?
Take it from me.
His personality flaws gave me adequate cause
To send him packing on a one-way trip
So his prospects take a terminal dip.
His assets frozen, the venue chosen
Is the ends of the earth, whoopee!
So long, ex-Prince Ali!